THE UNSEEN STRENGTH

UNVEILING THE POWER OF HIGHLY SENSITIVE INDIVIDUALS IN A RAPID AND OVERWHELMING WORLD

GODSWILL LEONARD

PREFACE

Welcome to "The Unseen Strength: Unveiling the Power of Highly Sensitive Individuals in a Rapid and Overwhelming World." In this exploration of the intricate tapestry of sensitivity, we embark on a journey to uncover the profound and often overlooked strengths that define Highly Sensitive Individuals (HSIs). The pages ahead delve into the depths of what it means to navigate a world that may not always fully comprehend the unique experiences of those with heightened sensitivity.

As we embark on this journey, it is essential to recognize the significance of understanding and embracing sensitivity as a strength rather than a limitation. Highly Sensitive Individuals possess a remarkable capacity for empathy, creativity, and depth of emotional experience. However, these qualities are often accompanied by challenges in a world that can be fast-paced, noisy, and overwhelming.

"The Unseen Strength" seeks to illuminate the hidden facets of sensitivity, bringing to light the resilience, creativity, and unique perspectives that flourish within HSIs. It serves as a guide for both those who identify as highly sensitive and those seeking a deeper understanding of the intricacies of sensitivity in a rapidly evolving world.

This book is not just an exploration of the challenges faced by HSIs but a celebration of their strengths. Through insightful narratives, practical strategies, and a holistic perspective, we aim to empower readers to embrace their own sensitivities or support those who navigate the world with heightened awareness.

As we navigate through the chapters, we invite you to reflect on the nuanced experiences of Highly Sensitive Individuals and the unseen strength that resides within them. Whether you are an HSI seeking validation and guidance or someone seeking to understand and support the highly sensitive individuals in your life, "The Unseen Strength" aims to provide insights, encouragement, and a sense of community.

Let the pages ahead be a source of inspiration, reflection, and empowerment. May this journey into the unseen strength within Highly Sensitive Individuals contribute to a greater appreciation of diversity, empathy, and authenticity in our interconnected world.

Warm regards,

[GODSWILL LEONARD]

DEDICATION

To all the Highly Sensitive Individuals who navigate the complexities of a rapid and overwhelming world with grace, resilience, and unwavering authenticity. Your unseen strength illuminates the path for others, inspiring understanding, empathy, and acceptance. May this book serve as a tribute to your unique experiences, a source of validation for your sensitivities, and a beacon of hope for your journey toward embracing the fullness of your authentic selves.

TABLE OF CONTENT

CHAPTER 1.

INTRODUCTION: EMBRACING SENSITIVITY IN A CHAOTIC WORLD

In a world that seems to move at an ever-increasing pace, where noise and stimuli surround us from every angle, the concept of sensitivity often finds itself at odds with the prevailing narrative of resilience and toughness. However, within this chaos lies a hidden power that often goes unnoticed – the strength of highly sensitive individuals. This introduction aims to set the stage for unraveling the layers of sensitivity, exploring its nuances, and ultimately embracing it as a profound asset in navigating the tumultuous landscape of the modern world.

The introductory chapter begins with a fundamental exploration of what it means to be a highly sensitive person. Delving beyond common misconceptions, it sheds light on the intricate nature of sensitivity, emphasizing that it is not a weakness but a unique trait that influences how individuals perceive and interact with their surroundings. By presenting sensitivity as a spectrum rather than a binary characteristic, readers are encouraged to appreciate the diversity within this group.

The narrative then pivots to the chaotic nature of the contemporary world. From the relentless pace of technological advancements to the constant barrage of information, the world can be overwhelming for many. Highly sensitive individuals, with their heightened awareness and depth of processing, may find themselves particularly susceptible to the challenges posed by this chaos. However, the introduction reframes this narrative, suggesting that sensitivity can be a beacon of strength amid the storm, allowing individuals to discern subtleties and navigate the complexities with a unique perspective.

One key aspect highlighted in the introduction is the emotional depth characteristic of highly sensitive individuals. This emotional richness, while occasionally perceived as vulnerability, is presented as a wellspring of strength. The ability to empathize deeply, connect authentically, and respond thoughtfully to emotions becomes a source of resilience in relationships and personal growth. The chapter prompts readers to reconsider traditional notions of strength, urging them to recognize the unseen power that lies within emotional intelligence.

As the introduction unfolds, it sets the tone for the journey ahead, promising a comprehensive exploration of the science behind sensitivity, practical strategies for thriving in various aspects of life, and ways to overcome the challenges inherent in being highly sensitive. The aim is not only to provide insights into the nature of sensitivity but to empower readers to embrace it fully.

In its concluding remarks, the introduction serves as an invitation. An invitation to embrace sensitivity not as a hindrance but as an unseen strength that can transform the way one experiences and contributes to the world. It lays the groundwork for a journey of self-discovery, resilience building, and empowerment for those who resonate with the label of highly sensitive individuals.

CHAPTER 2.

UNDERSTANDING THE HIGHLY SENSITIVE PERSON

Understanding the Highly Sensitive Person (HSP) delves into the intricacies of a personality trait that often stands at the intersection of perception and emotion. Highly Sensitive Persons possess a heightened sensitivity to stimuli, perceiving the world with a depth and intensity that sets them apart from the general population.

At the core of understanding an HSP is acknowledging that sensitivity is not synonymous with fragility. It's a spectrum, and individuals may fall anywhere along it. The trait is often characterized by a more finely tuned nervous system, making HSPs more receptive to sensory input. This heightened sensitivity can manifest in various ways, including a keen awareness of subtleties, a deep emotional responsiveness, and an acute sensitivity to environmental stimuli such as noise, light, or even social dynamics.

Key to understanding HSPs is recognizing that their responses to stimuli are not a choice but a natural part of their temperament. While someone else might easily brush off a loud noise, an HSP might find it overwhelming due to their enhanced sensory processing. It's essential to approach this understanding without judgment, appreciating the diversity in human temperament.

Empathy and compassion play crucial roles in grasping the essence of an HSP. Highly Sensitive Persons often have an exceptional capacity for empathy, feeling and understanding the emotions of others intensely. This emotional depth contributes to their unique interpersonal dynamics, fostering deeper connections but also requiring thoughtful consideration of their emotional well-being.

Moreover, understanding an HSP involves recognizing the impact of overstimulation. Highly sensitive individuals can easily become overwhelmed by excessive stimuli, leading to stress or burnout. Creating environments that allow for downtime and minimizing unnecessary stimuli can significantly contribute to their well-being.

The science behind sensitivity further elucidates the neurological aspects of being an HSP. Research suggests that the brains of HSPs exhibit heightened activity in areas associated with empathy, emotional processing, and sensory perception. This biological foundation underscores that sensitivity is not merely a personality quirk but has tangible roots in the structure and function of the nervous system.

To support HSPs effectively, it's crucial to foster environments that acknowledge and accommodate their unique needs. This might involve open communication about sensory preferences, creating quiet spaces, and understanding that downtime is not laziness but a necessity for their mental and emotional recharge.

In essence, understanding the Highly Sensitive Person is a journey of appreciation and acceptance. It involves acknowledging the beauty in their nuanced perception of the world, valuing their empathetic nature, and creating spaces that honor their unique sensitivities. By embracing the diversity of temperaments, we can cultivate environments where HSPs thrive, contributing their invaluable perspectives to the tapestry of human experience.

CHAPTER 3.

THE SCIENCE BEHIND SENSITIVITY: EXPLORING THE NEUROLOGY

Delving into "The Science Behind Sensitivity" unveils the fascinating realm of neurology that underlies the experiences of Highly Sensitive Persons (HSPs). At the core of this exploration is an understanding that sensitivity is not just a personality trait but a phenomenon rooted in the intricacies of the nervous system.

Research suggests that the brains of HSPs exhibit distinctive patterns of activity compared to non-HSPs. Neuroimaging studies have revealed heightened activity in regions associated with emotional processing, empathy, and sensory perception. The amygdala, a key player in processing emotions, tends to be more responsive in HSPs, contributing to their heightened emotional sensitivity.

Furthermore, the insula, a region involved in self-awareness and social emotions, shows increased activation in HSPs. This heightened activation in both the amygdala and insula contributes to the depth of emotional experience that characterizes highly sensitive individuals. They not only perceive emotions more intensely but also exhibit a heightened awareness of their own emotional states.

The mirror neuron system, responsible for empathy and understanding others' emotions, also plays a role in the science behind sensitivity. HSPs often display a heightened mirror neuron response, allowing them to deeply connect with the emotional experiences of those around them. This heightened empathy contributes to their ability to form strong emotional bonds and understand subtle social cues.

Additionally, the sensory processing sensitivity (SPS) theory, proposed by psychologist Elaine Aron, suggests that HSPs process sensory information more deeply due to a lower threshold for sensory stimulation. This heightened sensory processing is not limited to emotional stimuli but extends to various sensory modalities, such as sound, sight, and touch. It explains why HSPs may feel overwhelmed in environments with high levels of noise or bright lights.

Understanding the neurological foundations of sensitivity helps dispel misconceptions that sensitivity is merely a subjective or emotional response. Instead, it emphasizes that sensitivity is deeply rooted in the structure and function of the brain. This scientific understanding not only validates the experiences of HSPs but also provides a basis for creating supportive environments that consider their unique neurological makeup.

Moreover, recognizing the neurobiological aspects of sensitivity fosters a more empathetic and informed societal approach. Rather than viewing sensitivity as a weakness, society can appreciate it as a natural variation in human temperament, with tangible roots in neurobiology. This shift in perspective contributes to building a more inclusive and understanding community that embraces the diversity of neurological experiences.

In conclusion, exploring the neurology behind sensitivity unravels the intricate workings of the highly sensitive brain. It provides a scientific foundation for understanding the heightened emotional and sensory experiences of HSPs, emphasizing that sensitivity is not merely a personal preference but a neurological predisposition. This knowledge paves the way for creating environments that respect and accommodate the unique needs of highly sensitive individuals, fostering a society that values the richness of diverse neurological experiences.

CHAPTER 4.

NAVIGATING RELATIONSHIPS: INTERACTING WITH OTHERS AS A HIGHLY SENSITIVE INDIVIDUAL

Navigating relationships as a Highly Sensitive Individual (HSI) involves a delicate dance between the profound emotional depth that characterizes HSPs and the intricacies of interpersonal dynamics. Understanding and effectively managing relationships is a key aspect of embracing and thriving as a highly sensitive person.

Effective communication becomes a cornerstone when navigating relationships as an HSI. Expressing one's needs, preferences, and boundaries openly and honestly helps others understand the unique aspects of sensitivity. Clear communication fosters an environment where both parties feel heard and respected, paving the way for more meaningful connections.

HSIs often possess a remarkable capacity for empathy, allowing them to understand and resonate with others' emotions deeply. While this can contribute positively to relationships, it's essential to strike a balance. Being attuned to others' feelings is valuable, but HSIs should also ensure they don't absorb or internalize negative emotions excessively, maintaining healthy emotional boundaries.

Navigating relationships involves recognizing the significance of surrounding oneself with individuals who appreciate and understand sensitivity. Cultivating connections with people who respect the need for quiet moments, understand sensory sensitivities, and value emotional authenticity can create a supportive network that enhances the well-being of an HSI.

Maintaining a healthy balance between independence and connection is crucial for HSIs. While meaningful relationships are essential, it's equally important for highly sensitive individuals to have sufficient alone time for emotional and sensory replenishment. Communicating this need for solitude ensures that relationships flourish without compromising the HSI's well-being.

Conflicts are a natural part of any relationship, and for HSIs, navigating disagreements requires a nuanced approach. Addressing conflicts with sensitivity involves avoiding harsh language, allowing space for emotions to be expressed, and seeking resolution through understanding rather than confrontation. Emphasizing the importance of finding common ground helps build stronger, more resilient relationships.

Empowering others with an understanding of sensitivity is a proactive step in navigating relationships. HSIs can share insights about their temperament, explaining the nuances of heightened sensory processing and emotional depth. This educational approach fosters empathy and dispels misconceptions, contributing to more harmonious interactions.

Navigating relationships as an HSI involves practicing self-compassion. Understanding that sensitivity is a unique trait, not a flaw, allows individuals to embrace themselves fully. It's crucial for HSIs to prioritize self-care, recognizing when they need to step back, recharge, and engage in activities that bring them joy and relaxation.

In essence, navigating relationships as a Highly Sensitive Individual is a journey of understanding, communication, and self-acceptance. By embracing the unique qualities of sensitivity and fostering connections that align with one's needs, HSIs can cultivate fulfilling and enriching relationships that contribute positively to their overall well-being. It's about finding a balance that allows for deep connections without compromising the essence of being a highly sensitive person in a world that may not always fully comprehend the depth of their experiences.

CHAPTER 5.

HARNESSING EMOTIONAL INTELLIGENCE: UTILIZING SENSITIVITY AS A STRENGTH

Harnessing emotional intelligence is a pivotal aspect of utilizing sensitivity as a strength for Highly Sensitive Individuals (HSIs). Rather than viewing heightened sensitivity as a vulnerability, understanding and managing emotions effectively can empower HSIs to navigate the world with resilience and authenticity.

One of the hallmarks of HSIs is their profound emotional depth. Instead of shying away from this intensity, harnessing emotional intelligence involves embracing and understanding it. This means recognizing that emotions are valuable messengers, providing insights into one's needs, desires, and reactions. By acknowledging and processing emotions conscientiously, HSIs can harness their emotional depth to foster self-awareness and personal growth.

Empathy is a natural strength for HSIs, allowing them to connect with others on a deep emotional level. Harnessing emotional intelligence involves leveraging this empathy to build meaningful and supportive relationships. By actively listening, validating others' feelings, and demonstrating understanding, HSIs can create an empathetic environment that fosters connection and mutual understanding.

Understanding emotional triggers is crucial for HSIs in harnessing their emotional intelligence. Sensory stimuli and specific situations can evoke strong emotional responses, and being aware of these triggers enables proactive self-management. Whether it's a crowded environment or a particular type of noise, recognizing and addressing triggers empowers

HSIs to navigate challenging situations more effectively.

Emotional resilience is a key component of utilizing sensitivity as a strength. Rather than being overwhelmed by intense emotions, HSIs can develop strategies to bounce back from challenges. This involves cultivating a positive mindset, seeking support when needed, and adopting coping mechanisms such as mindfulness or grounding techniques. Building emotional resilience enables HSIs to face adversity with grace and adaptability.

Communication is central to emotional intelligence, and for HSIs, expressing emotions effectively is a skill worth honing. Articulating feelings with clarity and assertiveness allows HSIs to convey their needs and boundaries in relationships and various settings. By communicating openly, HSIs can ensure that their emotional experiences are understood, fostering healthier interactions with others.

While emotional intelligence emphasizes understanding and expressing emotions, it also involves balancing these emotions with rational thinking. HSIs can harness their sensitivity by integrating emotional and logical perspectives, making well-informed decisions that consider both aspects. Striking this balance ensures that sensitivity contributes to wise and thoughtful choices rather than impulsive reactions.

Harnessing emotional intelligence extends beyond personal relationships into professional and daily life. In the workplace, HSIs can use their heightened emotional awareness to excel in roles that require empathy, collaboration, and understanding. By recognizing and managing their own emotions and those of colleagues, HSIs contribute positively to team dynamics and organizational culture.

In personal life, emotional intelligence enables HSIs to navigate various social situations with grace and authenticity. Whether it's managing conflicts, building meaningful connections, or fostering self-growth, the ability to harness emotional intelligence transforms sensitivity from a potential challenge into a powerful asset.

In conclusion, utilizing sensitivity as a strength involves the intentional cultivation of emotional intelligence. By embracing emotional depth, cultivating empathy, recognizing triggers, developing resilience, expressing emotions effectively, and balancing logic with emotion, HSIs can navigate the world with authenticity and resilience. Ultimately, harnessing emotional intelligence empowers HSIs to not only understand themselves more deeply but also contribute positively to the relationships and communities they engage with.

CHAPTER 6.

THRIVING IN WORK AND CAREER: STRATEGIES FOR SUCCESS

Thriving in work and career as a Highly Sensitive Individual (HSI) involves navigating professional landscapes with an understanding of one's unique temperament. While the workplace can be challenging for HSIs due to stimuli and social dynamics, employing strategic approaches can transform sensitivity into a powerful asset for success.

One of the key strategies for thriving in work as an HSI is identifying and seeking out environments that align with one's sensitivities. Reflecting on personal preferences regarding noise levels, office design, and team dynamics helps HSIs choose workplaces that foster productivity and well-being. This proactive approach allows for a more harmonious integration of sensitivity into the professional sphere.

Thriving as an HSI often involves advocating for workplace accommodations that support sensory needs. This could include requesting a quieter workspace, using noise-canceling headphones, or negotiating flexible work arrangements. By communicating these needs respectfully, HSIs can create an environment that allows them to perform at their best, contributing to both personal fulfillment and professional success.

Emotional intelligence, a natural strength for HSIs, becomes a powerful tool in leadership roles. HSIs often excel in understanding and empathizing with others' emotions, making them effective leaders who can foster positive team dynamics. Leveraging emotional intelligence in leadership involves creating a supportive work culture, recognizing and valuing team members' contributions, and navigating conflicts with empathy and diplomacy.

Thriving in a demanding work environment requires effective time management and the establishment of clear boundaries. HSIs can prioritize tasks, break down projects into manageable steps, and schedule breaks to prevent sensory overload. Setting boundaries is crucial for maintaining a balance between work and personal life, ensuring that HSIs have the necessary time and space for rest and rejuvenation.

Open communication is fundamental for thriving in any work environment, and HSIs can benefit from cultivating transparent communication about their needs and preferences. This involves expressing sensitivities and discussing potential accommodations with supervisors or colleagues. By fostering open communication, HSIs contribute to a workplace culture that values diversity and individual well-being.

HSIs often possess heightened creativity and innovative thinking. Thriving in work involves recognizing and embracing these strengths, contributing fresh perspectives and problem-solving approaches. Employers increasingly value creativity as a key asset, and HSIs can leverage their unique insights to stand out and make meaningful contributions to their organizations.

Investing in continuous learning and professional development is a strategic approach for thriving in a dynamic work environment. HSIs can stay abreast of industry trends, acquire new skills, and participate in training programs that enhance their expertise. This commitment to growth not only ensures professional relevance but also boosts confidence and resilience in the face of challenges.

Building supportive networks within the workplace and industry is instrumental for success. Connecting with colleagues who understand and appreciate sensitivity can create a sense of camaraderie. Mentorship programs, industry events, and professional associations provide opportunities for networking, fostering a supportive community that can help HSIs navigate challenges and share insights.

In conclusion, thriving in work and career as a Highly Sensitive Individual involves a combination of self-awareness, proactive communication, and strategic decision-making. By identifying ideal work environments, advocating for accommodations, leveraging emotional intelligence in leadership, managing time effectively, fostering open communication, embracing creativity, investing in continuous learning, and building supportive networks, HSIs can transform their sensitivity into a powerful asset for professional success and personal fulfillment. It's about recognizing and valuing the unique strengths that sensitivity brings to the table, ultimately contributing to a more diverse, inclusive, and thriving professional landscape.

CHAPTER 7.

SELF-CARE PRACTICES FOR HIGHLY SENSITIVE INDIVIDUALS

Self-care is a vital component of well-being for anyone, but for Highly Sensitive Individuals (HSIs), it takes on special significance. With heightened sensitivity to stimuli and emotions, practicing self-care becomes a cornerstone for managing and thriving in the often overwhelming modern world.

Before delving into self-care practices, it's crucial for HSIs to recognize sensitivity as a strength rather than a weakness. Acceptance of this trait sets the foundation for intentional self-care. Sensitivity allows for a deep connection with emotions, heightened empathy, and a unique perspective that can be valuable in various aspects of life.

One key aspect of self-care for HSIs involves creating sensory-friendly environments. This could mean having a designated quiet space at home or work, using soft lighting, and incorporating calming elements like plants or soothing colors. These intentional adjustments help minimize sensory overload and provide a sanctuary for relaxation and rejuvenation.

HSIs thrive when they prioritize downtime and solitude. In a world that often values constant stimulation, taking intentional breaks becomes crucial. Whether it's a quiet walk, meditation, or simply spending time alone with a book, carving out moments for solitude allows HSIs to recharge their emotional and sensory batteries.

Self-care for HSIs involves setting and maintaining healthy boundaries. This includes saying no when necessary, communicating limits to friends and colleagues, and recognizing when to step back from overwhelming situations. Establishing clear boundaries helps prevent burnout and ensures that HSIs can engage with the world at their own pace and comfort level.

Mindfulness practices, such as meditation and deep-breathing exercises, are powerful tools for HSIs. These techniques promote present-moment awareness, helping individuals manage stress and anxiety. Regular mindfulness practice enhances emotional regulation and cultivates a sense of calm amidst the external chaos, making it an invaluable self-care strategy.

Physical well-being is intricately connected to mental and emotional health. Engaging in regular exercise, maintaining a balanced diet, and prioritizing sufficient sleep contribute to overall vitality. Physical self-care not only supports HSIs in managing stress but also enhances their resilience to external pressures.

For many HSIs, engaging in creative pursuits is a form of self-care. Whether it's art, writing, music, or any other creative outlet, expressing oneself allows for emotional release and a sense of accomplishment. Creative endeavors become a channel for processing intense emotions and connecting with one's inner self.

Surrounding oneself with a supportive social network is a crucial aspect of self-care. Building connections with individuals who understand and appreciate sensitivity fosters a sense of belonging. Supportive friends and family provide a safe space for HSIs to share experiences, seek advice, and receive emotional validation.

Engaging in therapeutic practices, such as counseling or psychotherapy, can be particularly beneficial for HSIs. These practices provide a structured space for self-reflection, emotional exploration, and skill-building. Therapeutic interventions equip HSIs with tools to navigate challenges, enhance resilience, and develop strategies for effective self-care.

Self-care for HSIs involves cultivating a positive mindset. This includes practicing self-compassion, challenging negative self-talk, and celebrating achievements, no matter how small. A positive mindset enhances overall well-being and contributes to a resilient and empowered approach to life.

In conclusion, self-care practices for Highly Sensitive Individuals are multifaceted and tailored to address the unique needs of sensitivity. By recognizing sensitivity as a strength, creating sensory-friendly environments, prioritizing downtime, establishing healthy boundaries, engaging in mindfulness, nurturing physical health, expressing creativity, building a supportive social network, participating in therapeutic practices, and cultivating a positive mindset, HSIs can foster a holistic approach to self-care. Ultimately, self-care becomes not just a necessity but a transformative journey of self-discovery, self-acceptance, and sustainable well-being in a world that may not always understand the depth of their experiences.

CHAPTER 8.

OVERCOMING CHALLENGES: COPING WITH OVERSTIMULATION AND BURNOUT

For Highly Sensitive Individuals (HSIs), overcoming challenges related to overstimulation and burnout is a crucial aspect of maintaining well-being in a world that often seems too loud, fast, and overwhelming. The heightened sensitivity to stimuli and emotions can lead to a higher risk of burnout, making it essential for HSIs to develop coping strategies to navigate these challenges successfully.

The first step in overcoming overstimulation and burnout is recognizing the triggers. HSIs often have specific triggers, whether they be crowded environments, loud noises, or prolonged social interactions. Identifying these triggers allows individuals to proactively set limits. It might involve knowing when to step back from a social gathering, taking breaks during a busy day, or creating designated quiet spaces to retreat to when needed.

Consistent and intentional self-care is a powerful tool in overcoming challenges associated with overstimulation and burnout. Establishing self-care routines that address physical, emotional, and sensory needs is essential. This could include regular breaks, engaging in calming activities, getting sufficient sleep, and incorporating mindfulness practices. By making self-care a priority, HSIs build resilience and create a buffer against the stressors that contribute to burnout.

Building a supportive environment is key to overcoming challenges. This involves communicating openly with friends, family, and colleagues about sensitivity and specific needs. Creating a network of understanding individuals who respect boundaries and offer support during challenging times is invaluable. A supportive environment fosters a sense of safety and understanding, reducing the risk of burnout.

HSIs benefit from developing effective stress management techniques to cope with overstimulation. These techniques may include deep-breathing exercises, progressive muscle relaxation, or guided imagery. The goal is to have a toolkit of strategies that can be easily accessed in moments of heightened stress. Regular practice enhances the effectiveness of these techniques, making them reliable tools for overcoming challenges.

Proactive time management is crucial for preventing burnout. HSIs may find it helpful to break tasks into smaller, more manageable steps and prioritize them based on importance. This approach prevents overwhelming workloads and allows for breaks between tasks. Time management strategies also include scheduling downtime and creating a balance between productivity and rest.

Overcoming challenges involves setting realistic expectations for oneself. HSIs may tend to set high standards, and while ambition is commendable, it's essential to strike a balance. Setting achievable goals and recognizing personal limits prevents burnout caused by unrealistic expectations. It's crucial to celebrate small victories and acknowledge that progress is often more important than perfection.

Mindful awareness is a powerful tool for HSIs in overcoming challenges related to overstimulation. Being present in the moment and fully engaging with the current experience allows individuals to navigate stimuli with greater ease. Mindfulness practices, such as meditation or mindful walking, enhance the ability to respond to external factors with calmness and resilience.

When challenges become overwhelming, seeking professional support is a proactive step. Therapists or counselors with experience in working with highly sensitive individuals can provide coping strategies, offer validation, and guide individuals through the process of overcoming burnout. Professional support reinforces the importance of mental health and well-being.

Embracing a growth mindset is a transformative approach to overcoming challenges. Viewing setbacks as opportunities for learning and growth shifts the perspective from a fixed mindset to one that is adaptive and resilient. This mindset fosters a positive outlook, encouraging HSIs to approach challenges as stepping stones rather than insurmountable obstacles.

In conclusion, overcoming challenges related to overstimulation and burnout is an ongoing journey for Highly Sensitive Individuals. By recognizing triggers, prioritizing self-care, creating a supportive environment, developing stress management techniques, implementing time management strategies, setting realistic expectations, practicing mindful awareness, seeking professional support, and embracing a growth mindset, HSIs can navigate the complexities of their sensitivity with resilience and a sense of empowerment. It's about cultivating a holistic approach that addresses the unique needs of sensitivity and transforms challenges into opportunities for personal growth and well-being.

CHAPTER 9.

CULTIVATING RESILIENCE: BUILDING INNER STRENGTH

Cultivating resilience is a transformative process that involves building inner strength to navigate challenges, setbacks, and the inevitable complexities of life. For Highly Sensitive Individuals (HSIs), resilience is particularly vital, as their heightened sensitivity may make them more susceptible to stressors. By consciously developing resilience, HSIs can enhance their ability to bounce back from adversity, maintain emotional well-being, and embrace the full spectrum of their experiences.

Resilience is not an inherent trait but a set of skills and attitudes that can be cultivated over time. It involves the ability to adapt to adversity, maintain equilibrium in the face of challenges, and recover from setbacks. For HSIs, resilience becomes a beacon of strength, allowing them to navigate a world that may not always align with their unique sensitivities.

Cultivating resilience begins with fostering a positive mindset. This involves reframing challenges as opportunities for growth, learning, and self-discovery. Instead of viewing setbacks as insurmountable obstacles, HSIs can approach them with a mindset that embraces the potential for resilience-building experiences. A positive outlook provides the foundation for overcoming adversity with grace and strength.

Emotional regulation is a key component of resilience. HSIs, with their heightened emotional responses, benefit from developing skills to navigate intense feelings effectively. This might include mindfulness practices, deep-breathing exercises, or journaling to process and understand emotions. By mastering emotional regulation, HSIs can respond to challenges with clarity and composure.

Self-compassion is a cornerstone of resilience. HSIs often have high expectations of themselves, and in times of difficulty, self-compassion becomes a source of inner strength. Being kind and understanding toward oneself, especially during challenging moments, fosters resilience by providing a supportive internal dialogue and promoting a sense of self-worth.

Resilience is often bolstered by a supportive social network. For HSIs, connecting with understanding friends, family, or like-minded individuals creates a safety net during challenging times. Sharing experiences, seeking advice, and receiving emotional support from others contribute significantly to building resilience. A supportive community reinforces the idea that challenges are shared aspects of the human experience.

Setting realistic goals and expectations is crucial for building resilience. HSIs may have a tendency to set high standards for themselves, and while ambition is commendable, it's essential to strike a balance. Realistic goals allow for a sense of achievement without overwhelming stress, fostering a positive cycle that contributes to resilience.

Resilience thrives in an environment of flexibility and adaptability. HSIs can cultivate resilience by developing the ability to adjust their responses to changing circumstances. This might involve adapting strategies, seeking alternative solutions, or reframing perspectives. Embracing flexibility enables HSIs to navigate uncertainties with a sense of empowerment rather than anxiety.

Each challenge presents an opportunity for learning and growth. Cultivating resilience involves extracting lessons from adversity, identifying strengths, and recognizing personal achievements in overcoming obstacles. By reframing setbacks as stepping stones, HSIs can build a reservoir of resilience that grows with each experience.

Resilience doesn't mean facing challenges alone. Seeking professional support, such as therapy or counseling, is a proactive step in building inner strength. Professionals can provide guidance, offer tools for resilience, and create a supportive space for HSIs to explore and navigate their unique experiences. Professional support reinforces the importance of prioritizing mental health and well-being.

In conclusion, cultivating resilience for Highly Sensitive Individuals is a multifaceted journey that involves fostering a positive mindset, developing emotional regulation skills, cultivating self-compassion, building a supportive social network, setting realistic goals, embracing flexibility, learning from adversity, and seeking professional support when needed. It's about recognizing the inherent strength within sensitivity, transforming challenges into opportunities for growth, and developing the inner fortitude to navigate the world with resilience and authenticity. Building resilience is not a destination but an ongoing process that empowers HSIs to face life's uncertainties with courage, adaptability, and a deep sense of inner strength.

CHAPTER 10.

EMBRACING YOUR AUTHENTIC SELF: LIVING FULLY AS A HIGHLY SENSITIVE PERSON

Embracing your authentic self as a Highly Sensitive Person (HSP) is a profound journey that involves acknowledging, celebrating, and fully integrating the unique aspects of your sensitivity into your life. Living authentically as an HSP requires self-acceptance, self-compassion, and the courage to navigate a world that may not always fully understand the depth of your experiences.

The first step in embracing your authentic self as an HSP is recognizing the inherent strength within sensitivity. Sensitivity is not a flaw but a unique trait that contributes depth, empathy, and a nuanced perspective to your interactions with the world. Understanding sensitivity as a strength rather than a weakness lays the foundation for living authentically.

Living fully as an HSP involves cultivating self-acceptance. This includes embracing your sensitivities, acknowledging your needs for solitude and reflection, and recognizing that your responses to stimuli are natural expressions of your temperament. Self-acceptance allows you to navigate the world authentically, free from the constraints of societal expectations or judgments.

Embracing your authentic self requires setting boundaries and prioritizing your well-being. This may involve communicating your needs to friends, family, and colleagues, advocating for sensory-friendly environments, and recognizing when to step back and recharge. Setting and maintaining healthy boundaries allow you to honor your authentic needs while engaging with the world on your own terms.

Living authentically involves expressing your creativity and individuality as an HSP. Whether through artistic pursuits, unique hobbies, or unconventional perspectives, embracing your authentic self allows you to celebrate the richness of your inner world. Expressing your creativity becomes a means of sharing your authentic self with the world, contributing your unique insights and experiences.

Authentic connections with others are a vital aspect of living fully as an HSP. Building relationships with individuals who appreciate and understand your sensitivity fosters a sense of belonging. Authentic connections provide a support system, enabling you to share your experiences, challenges, and triumphs with those who value and respect your authentic self.

Embracing your authentic self involves honoring your intuition and emotional depth. As an HSP, your heightened sensitivity allows for a deep connection with your emotions and an intuitive understanding of the world. Trusting and honoring these aspects of yourself leads to more authentic decision-making and a richer, more meaningful experience of life.

Living authentically as an HSP often involves practicing mindful awareness. Being present in the moment, fully engaging with your surroundings, and embracing the depth of your emotional experiences allow you to navigate the world with authenticity. Mindful awareness fosters a deeper connection with your authentic self, promoting self-discovery and self-expression.

Embracing your authentic self is an ongoing process, and celebrating small victories and progress is essential. Recognize and acknowledge moments of authenticity, courage, and self-discovery. Cultivating a positive mindset that values growth and self-acceptance reinforces your commitment to living fully as an HSP.

Living authentically may come with challenges, and seeking support and guidance is a proactive step. Whether through therapy, counseling, or joining supportive communities, reaching out to those who understand the HSP experience provides validation and encouragement on your journey toward embracing your authentic self.

In conclusion, embracing your authentic self as a Highly Sensitive Person is a transformative and empowering journey. It involves recognizing the strength in sensitivity, cultivating self-acceptance, setting boundaries, expressing creativity, building authentic connections, honoring intuition, practicing mindful awareness, celebrating small victories, and seeking support when needed. Living authentically as an HSP is about navigating the world with authenticity, courage, and a deep appreciation for the richness that sensitivity brings to every aspect of your life. It's a journey of self-discovery, self-acceptance, and the ongoing celebration of your unique and authentic self.

CHAPTER 11.

CONCLUSION: EMBRACING THE UNSEEN STRENGTH WITHIN YOU

In the journey of embracing the unseen strength within you, the recognition and celebration of your unique qualities as a Highly Sensitive Person (HSP) become pivotal. This concluding chapter is an opportunity to reflect on the transformative power of acknowledging, valuing, and fully integrating the strengths that may not always be visible to the outside world.

Embracing the unseen strength within you begins with self-discovery. As an HSP, understanding the intricacies of your temperament, the depth of your emotions, and the unique lens through which you perceive the world lay the foundation for embracing authenticity. Self-discovery is an ongoing process that unfolds layers of your identity, empowering you to recognize the inherent strength that resides within your sensitivities.

The journey of self-discovery, as an HSP, equips you with resilience in navigating challenges. Whether it's managing overstimulation, setting boundaries, or seeking support when needed, the resilience cultivated through self-awareness becomes a source of inner strength. Challenges are transformed into opportunities for growth, learning, and a deeper understanding of your own capacities.

Embracing the unseen strength within you involves recognizing the beauty in sensitivity. Your heightened emotional depth, empathetic nature, and creative insights contribute to the richness of your experiences. Sensitivity is not a burden to be carried but a gift that enhances your capacity for connection, understanding, and a profound appreciation for the intricacies of life.

Living authentically as an HSP requires courage. It's the courage to set boundaries in a world that may not always understand your needs. It's the courage to express your creativity, individuality, and unique perspectives boldly. Embracing the unseen strength within you involves stepping into the authenticity of who you are, despite external pressures or societal expectations.

Central to embracing the unseen strength within you is the practice of self-compassion. Recognizing that sensitivity is not a weakness but a fundamental aspect of your being allows for a kind and understanding relationship with yourself. Self-compassion becomes a guiding light, fostering resilience, self-acceptance, and a gentle acknowledgment of your journey's complexities.

The journey of embracing unseen strength is not a solitary one. It involves building connections and seeking support from those who understand and appreciate the HSP experience. Authentic relationships provide a sense of belonging, understanding, and encouragement. The power of shared experiences and supportive communities becomes a vital resource on your path to embracing the unseen strength within you.

As you continue to embrace the unseen strength within you, take time to celebrate the growth and progress made along the way. Every step, no matter how small, contributes to the evolution of your authentic self. Acknowledge the courage it takes to navigate a world that may not always align with your sensitivities and recognize the strides made in embracing your unique strengths.

Embracing the unseen strength within you is not a destination but a lifelong journey. It involves continuous self-discovery, self-compassion, and the commitment to living authentically. The unseen strength within you is dynamic, evolving, and resilient. It propels you forward, encouraging you to embrace the fullness of your experiences and navigate the world with a profound understanding of the strength that lies within your sensitivity.

As you conclude this chapter of embracing the unseen strength within you, carry forward the lessons learned, the resilience cultivated, and the authenticity embraced. Your journey as a Highly Sensitive Person is a testament to the unseen strength that shapes your unique identity. Embrace it, celebrate it, and continue to navigate the world with the courage and wisdom that comes from recognizing the unseen strength within you.

www.ingramcontent.com/pod-product-compliance
Lightning Source LLC
Chambersburg PA
CBHW070439290526
45791CB00005B/2041